WITH HARP AND SLING   116

The Shepherd Boy Who Became a King,
   1 Samuel 16: 1-13   118
A Special Person's Special Work,
   A Muffin Family Story   121

A Harp for the King, *1 Samuel 16: 14-23*   124
Sweet Music, *A Muffin Family Story*   128

The Little Stone That Won a Battle,
   1 Samuel 17: 1-53   132
Big Bill Bluffalo, *A Muffin Family Story*   136

Good Friends, *1 Samuel 17: 55–18: 4*   140
The Friend I Never Saw, *A Muffin Family Story*   142

MINI'S WORD LIST   144

TO PARENTS AND TEACHERS

Each child has some special place where stories build a bridge between fantasy and reality, yesterday and today, a world that was in Bible times and the world that is along Main Street. You, the parent or teacher, may remember such a place from your childhood where Mother, Father, or teacher whisked you away to magic kingdoms through stories. It may have been a fluffy rug where you sat to listen or a big chair where Mother or Father read to you. Or it may have been your own certain place.

The Tagalong Tree is that kind of place, and those who sit under it may enter the exciting world of stories, both then and now. In a previous volume, *Through Golden Windows*, your child began his adventures with the Muffin family. Now, with *Under the Tagalong Tree*, he will renew old friendships with Maxi, Mini, Mommi, Poppi, Ruff and Tuff, and others.

The Bible stories are retold from the Scriptures, so you may wish to use the Bible itself as your children share in the adventures of this volume.

Under the Tagalong Tree

By V. Gilbert Beers

Illustrated by Helen Endres

MOODY PRESS • CHICAGO

What You Will Find in This Book

Library of Congress Cataloging in Publication Data

Beers, Victor Gilbert, 1928-
    Under the tagalong tree.

    SUMMARY: A number of Bible stories that are followed by tales involving the Muffin family which illustrate the contemporary application of Biblical principles.

    1. Bible stories, English. [1. Bible stories. 2. Christian life]. I. Endres, Helen. II. Title.

BS551.2.B45   220.9'505   76-22173

ISBN 0-8024-9021-2

Printed in the United States of America

STORIES OF LONG AGO — 4

When the World Was Made, *Genesis 1–2: 3, 18-25* — 6
Big, Big Birds and Little Purple Puddles,
    A Muffin Family Story — 10

Don't Eat That! *Genesis 3* — 14
Mrs. Fry's Pies, *A Muffin Family Story* — 18

Who Sent the Rain? *Genesis 6: 5–9: 17* — 24
Mini Muffin's Marvelous Muffins,
    A Muffin Family Story — 27

The Tower Builders, *Genesis 11: 1-9* — 32
The Great Play House, *A Muffin Family Story* — 35

CHILDREN JESUS KNEW — 40

Stop Crying! *Luke 7: 11-17* — 42
If I Could Do Anything, *A Muffin Family Story* — 45

Too Late Is Never Too Late, *Luke 8: 41-42, 49-56* — 48
That Dumb Cat, *A Muffin Family Story* — 51

The Man Who Is Never Too Busy, *Mark 10: 13-16* — 56
The Newspaper, *A Muffin Family Story* — 60

If You Want to Be First, *Matthew 18: 1-10* — 64
I'm First, *A Muffin Family Story* — 68

THE ORPHAN QUEEN — 72

The Orphan Queen, *Esther 2: 1-20* — 74
Tuff Luck, *A Muffin Family Story* — 77

Sealed with the King's Ring, *Esther 3* — 80
Better than a Best Friend, *A Muffin Family Story* — 83

A Brave Queen Who Saved Her People, *Esther 4–9* — 86
A Very Wet Walk, *A Muffin Family Story* — 90

COURAGE WITH KINGS AND SHIPWRECKS — 94

Telling Someone About a Friend, *Acts 25: 13–26:32* — 96
Mayor McBroom, *A Muffin Family Story* — 99

Shipwreck! *Acts 27* — 102
Play Ball! *A Muffin Family Story* — 106

The Man Who Was Not Afraid, *Acts 28* — 110
Barking Dogs and Banana Peelings,
    A Muffin Family Story — 113

STORIES OF LONG AGO

When the World Was Made

GENESIS 1—2:3,18-25

At first, the world was not a bright, beautiful ball, shining in the sunlight. It was a dark, gloomy place, with no shape or form. There was no sun or moon to light the skies, and no stars to twinkle in the darkness.

There was nothing but darkness everywhere. Only in heaven, God's home, was there a bright happy place.

"Let there be light!" God said one day. So light appeared on the earth. God called the light time day and the dark time night.

"Now let the skies and the seas each find its place," God said. So the great waters swirled below and formed the seas. The skies appeared above them. From the seas, great islands of land arose. The land dried and God named it earth.

"Let grass and plants and trees grow from the earth," God said. When He spoke, beautiful things began to grow and soon the earth was covered with soft grass, green plants, and trees filled with good fruit to eat. God was pleased with all the lovely things that He had made.

"Let lights appear in the skies," God commanded. God made two big lights, one to shine in the day and the other to shine at night. He called the light for the day the sun, and the light for the night He called the moon. He also made stars to shine at night, to fill the skies with twinkling lights.

God was pleased with His bright, beautiful world. But He wanted something more.

"Let the waters come alive with fish, and the skies with birds," God said. Fish began to swim in the waters and the skies came alive with beautiful birds.

"Now let cattle and lizards, and snakes and other animals come alive upon the earth," God said. God made all kinds of wonderful animals to fill the earth. There were cattle to walk upon the hills, snakes and lizards to crawl upon the ground, and other animals to run here and there among the plants and trees.

"But there is something else the world needs," God said. "I will make someone to be like Me. He can love Me, and talk with Me, and work for Me."

So God made someone to be like Himself. He called that someone man. He also made a woman to live with the man so they could take care of each other and help each other and have children.

God was so happy with the wonderful things that He had made. At last He rested, for it was the seventh day. God blessed the seventh day and made it a special day when we can do special things for Him.

The man was named Adam. The woman was Eve. "She will be the mother of all people who live on this earth," said Adam.

Adam and Eve loved their beautiful home that God had made. They loved to talk with God and take care of the wonderful things that He had made. And God gave them everything that they needed.

WHAT DO YOU THINK?

1. What kind of a world did God make for us? How do you think He wants us to take care of it? What do you think of the way men have cared for God's wonderful world?

2. How much did God provide for Adam and Eve in the home He made for them? What do you think they said to God when they talked to Him?

Big, Big Birds
and Little Purple Puddles

Mommi Muffin must have told Maxi a dozen times or more not to throw his coat in the corner. Today it was his yellow raincoat.

"Yuk!" Maxi grumbled. "Why does it have to rain?"

"Because God planned it that way," Mommi called from the kitchen.

"Couldn't God think of a better way?" Maxi complained.

"Maxi!" shouted Mini Muffin. "Shame on you. Don't say such things. I suppose you could have planned things better than God did."

Maxi tossed his school books on a table and ran to the kitchen to get a snack. "Just a few things," he called back to Mini.

"Like what?" Mini asked as she followed Maxi into the kitchen.

Maxi munched on a cookie as he thought awhile. "Well," said Maxi. That always seemed like a safe way for Maxi to begin. Nobody could argue with that. "If God had to make rain, why didn't He make it some pretty color, like—well, like purple?"

"Purple rain?" Mommi asked. "Are you sure?"

"Yuk," said Mini. "Think of splashing in purple puddles."

But Maxi went on with his plans for the world. "And do you see those poor little birds outside?" he asked. "How would you like to be a little bird and have all those big cats chase you?"

"Maxi! You'll hurt Tuff's feelings," Mini shouted. "Don't you love Tuff?"

"Of course," said Maxi. "But I wouldn't if I were a little bird. I think God should have made birds BIG. Then they could take care of themselves."

Maxi and Mini talked about the purple rain and the big birds more after supper. When Mini told Poppi what Maxi said, Poppi frowned. "Hmmm," he said. "Purple rain and big birds. My, what a world that would be."

11

Maxi fell asleep thinking of the purple rain and the big birds. Suddenly, in his dream, it began to rain. "Look!" Maxi shouted. "It's purple! Isn't that beautiful?"

Maxi put on his yellow raincoat and went out to play in the purple puddles. Soon he was covered with the purple rain. But when Maxi tried to come back inside, Mommi met him at the door.

"Don't you come in here with that purple stuff all over you," said Mommi. "You'll have to stay outside."

But Maxi was cold and purple all over. He wanted to come inside. "Dumb purple rain," Maxi complained as he splashed in some purple puddles. "I can't even go inside my own house."

Just then Maxi heard a strange noise. It sounded like wings, but it was such a BIG noise. Then Maxi looked up. There was a BIG, BIG bird flying down toward him. Maxi had never seen such a big bird. It was bigger than a horse.

The BIG, BIG bird swooped down and grabbed Maxi in its claws. Then it began to fly up through the purple rain.

"Put me down!" Maxi cried out. "PUT ME DOWN! PUT ME DOWN! PUT—"

Just then Maxi opened his eyes and looked up. There was Mini Muffin, staring at him. He was back in his own room. It was all a dream.

"I can't put you down," said Mini. "I never picked you up. But please hurry and get up so we can splash in the puddles. It rained last night."

"Are they purple?" Maxi asked.

"No, silly, they're rain colored," Mini giggled.

"Hooray!" Maxi shouted. "God made them the right color after all. And look at that cute little bird in the tree outside."

"What happened to you?" Mini asked. "I thought you liked big birds and purple puddles."

"Not now," said Maxi. "It's something a little bird, I mean a big bird, told me."

LET'S TALK ABOUT THIS

1. Have you ever thought you could have planned things better than God did? What did Maxi think about this?

2. What changed Maxi's mind about purple puddles and big birds?

3. Think of all the wonderful ways that God has planned His world. Why not thank Him now for all His good gifts? Aren't you really glad He made things the way they are?

Don't Eat That!

GENESIS 3

"It's all yours," God told Adam and Eve. "You may have anything in the Garden of Eden. But you must not eat the fruit on that tree! It would not be good for you."

That tree was so beautiful!

And the fruit looked so good!

But Adam and Eve wouldn't eat the fruit, for God had said that they should not eat it. Of course, Adam often stopped to admire the beautiful fruit. And Eve usually went that way when she walked through the garden.

One day Eve walked past the beautiful tree. As usual, she stopped to look at it.

"It is a beautiful tree," she whispered softly. "And the fruit looks so good."

"It is good," a voice answered from the tree. "You should try some."

Eve was surprised to hear a voice speaking from the tree. Then she saw a big snake. The voice was coming from the snake.

"I can't eat that fruit," Eve said. "God told Adam not to eat it."

"Did God really say that?" the snake questioned.

"Yes," said Eve. "He said that we would die if we ate this fruit."

The snake chuckled. "God knows that you won't die!" he said. "That fruit will make you wise. You will be like God, for you will know good and evil."

Eve looked and looked at the fruit. Just think! She could be like God. Adam could, too! She had never heard of good and evil before. It sounded like fun to know more about that.

Suddenly Eve reached out and touched a piece of fruit. Her hand began to tremble. Why did she feel the way she did? She wanted to eat the fruit more than anything else in the garden. But she felt bad doing it, for God had told her not to eat it.

At last Eve put the fruit to her mouth. "Oh, this is good," she shouted. "I must give some to Adam. He will love it!"

Before long, Adam and Eve knew things they had never known before. They knew that they had no clothes and were ashamed. So they put some leaves together to wear.

That evening they heard God coming to visit them in the garden. But they did not want to talk with God. They were ashamed, for they had disobeyed Him.

"Why are you hiding from Me?" God called to Adam.

"Because I'm not wearing any clothes," Adam answered. "I'm ashamed for You to see me without clothes."

"How did you come to know that you have no clothes?" God asked. "Did you eat from that tree?"

Adam was afraid. God knew! "Eve gave me the fruit," he complained.

"Why did you do that?" God asked Eve.

"It was the snake," Eve answered. "He made me do it."

"Then you must crawl on the ground from now on," God told the snake. "You and Eve's children will always be afraid of each other."

God scolded Eve next. "You will hurt whenever you have a baby," He said. "And you, Adam, will work to get your food from now on. You will have thistles and thorns in your garden and you will sweat as you work the ground. Then when you die, you will go back into the ground again."

God gave Adam and Eve some animal skins to wear. "Now you must leave the Garden of Eden," He said. "You will never come back."

Adam and Eve looked back as they left the garden. They would never live in their beautiful home again. They were sorry now that they had not obeyed God. They were sorry that they had eaten the fruit of that tree.

WHAT DO YOU THINK?

1. Why didn't Adam and Eve do what God told them? Why did they eat the fruit when they already had everything they needed?

2. What does it mean to be tempted? How was Eve tempted?

3. What happened to Adam and Eve when they disobeyed God? How did that change their lives?

Mrs. Fry's Pies

"Ummmm! What's that wonderful smell?" Pookie's friends asked. Everyone stopped playing catch and began to sniff the air. "Huh? What is it Pookie?"

"Mrs. Fry's pies!" said Pookie. "She bakes the most wonderful pies for Mr. Fry's Pie Shop."

"Would she give us some pie to eat?" Maxi Muffin asked.

"I don't know," said Pookie. "I just know that she puts some of them on a shelf on the other side of the fence."

"Why does she do that?" asked Mini Muffin.

Pookie chuckled. "She told my mom that pies taste better when they cool outside," said Pookie. "But my mom says she never heard of that before. Anyway, that's how she does it and everyone says her pies are great."

19

Pookie and his friends tried to play catch again while Mini watched. But the wonderful smell of Mrs. Fry's pies became more wonderful all the time.

Suddenly BoBo threw his mitt on the ground. "I'm going to have some pie!" he said. "It just smells too good."

"But how?" asked Pookie.

"You'll see!" said BoBo. "Watch me!"

First, BoBo pushed the picnic table near the board fence. Then he put the benches on top of the table.

"Now for the final act in my Great Pie Plan," said BoBo as he put a lawn chair on top of the benches.

"You shouldn't be doing this, you know," said Mini Muffin.

"Mini's right, BoBo," said Pookie. "I don't like it."

But BoBo was already up on top of the lawn chair, reaching over the board fence for a pie.

"Blueberry!" BoBo shouted, holding the pie up as he said it. But just as BoBo said that, the lawn chair began to wobble.

"Yike!" shouted BoBo. The lawn chair wobbled some more. Then BoBo and the lawn chair came tumbling to the ground.

The blueberry pie came tumbling down, too, right on BoBo.

"Ohhhh," said Mini.

"Blueberry BoBo!" Pookie laughed. He thought it was funny, but none of his friends laughed. BoBo certainly didn't.

Just then Pookie and his friends heard a voice. "I saw that!" the voice said. Then they saw Mrs. Fry, looking over the fence at them.

"I saw the whole thing!" said Mrs. Fry. "You children come right over here."

"Now we're going to get it," said Maxi Muffin. "It's all your fault, BoBo."

So Pookie and his friends marched slowly around the board fence to Mrs. Fry's back yard. Blueberry BoBo came last, with blueberry pie still dripping from him.

"Those pies are such a temptation," said Mrs. Fry when the friends all arrived. "I really shouldn't put them there."

Pookie and his friends hung their heads. They hadn't done anything. It was BoBo. But what could they say?

"I heard you playing ball over there," said Mrs. Fry. "So I baked two blueberry pies for you. Your blueberry friend has one of them. The rest of you can have the other, with ice cream on it."

"I'm sorry, I really am," said BoBo. "I know it was wrong to take your pie."

"I'm glad that you're sorry," said Mrs. Fry. "Now, how about a big dish of ice cream?"

"Mrs. Fry's pies really ARE good!" said Pookie and his friends.

"Yeah, they really are," said Blueberry BoBo as he licked some pie from his finger.

Everyone laughed at that, even Mrs. Fry and Blueberry BoBo himself.

LET'S TALK ABOUT THIS

1. How was BoBo tempted? What did he do when he was tempted?

2. Have you been tempted to do something wrong this week? What did you do? Did you do what you wanted or what God wanted?

3. What should you do when you are tempted? Why should you talk to God and His friends then?

4. If you do something wrong when you are tempted, what should you do then? What did BoBo do? What will God do if you tell Him you are sorry?

Who Sent the Rain?

GENESIS 6:5—9:17

"I'm sorry I made them," said the Lord.

Wherever He looked, the Lord saw people doing things they shouldn't do. Nobody tried to please Him. Nobody but Noah.

"Why don't the others try to please Me as Noah does?" God asked. "I'm sorry that I made them. I will take all of them from the earth, all except Noah and his family."

The Lord talked with Noah about these things. "You must make a boat the way I tell you," said the Lord. "When you are finished, I will send a flood to destroy everything. But you and your family will be inside the big boat. You will also have animals in the boat."

Noah did exactly what the Lord told him to do. He built the boat from wood as the Lord said. Day after day, he worked on the boat, along with the men who worked with him.

"What are you doing?" his neighbors asked.

"Making a boat," Noah answered.

"Here? But there is no water here," they said.

"There will be," said Noah. "God will send a big flood some day. Those who are inside our big boat will be safe. The others will drown."

The neighbors laughed and laughed. There had never been much rain around there. It was so funny to think of a flood in the desert.

People kept laughing at Noah and his big boat. But Noah kept making the boat. This went on for a hundred and twenty years. Most people would have given up. But not Noah. He believed what God had said. He knew that God would never lie to him.

"There will be a big flood," said Noah. "God said so." Noah kept working until the boat was finished.

One day God spoke to Noah. "Go into the boat with your family," He said. "Take the animals and birds that I tell you."

So Noah went into the big boat with his family. He took the animals and birds that God told him to take.

Noah's neighbors had come to see all the excitement. They were sure now that Noah was crazy. Look at him driving all those animals on his big boat!

But while they watched, the sky grew dark. When God closed the big door of the boat, the rain began to fall.

"Rain!" some people shouted. The people were terrified as the rain began to pour down. Soon the water swirled around their feet, then rose higher and higher.

"Let us in!" the people cried. They pounded on the door of the big boat. But it was too late. The door was closed and could not be opened now.

All through the day the rain poured down. It rained all night and the next day, too. The rain kept on falling. Soon the earth was covered with water. But Noah and his family were safe inside the big boat.

"God did send the flood, just as He promised," said Noah's family.

"God always keeps His promises," Noah said. "And we must keep our promises to Him, too."

WHAT DO YOU THINK?

1. How do you think Noah and his family felt when they worked for a hundred and twenty years on a boat in the desert? Do you think they sometimes wondered if it would rain enough to use it?

2. Why had God told them to make this boat? Why would they need it? Why did this seem strange in the dry land where they lived?

3. How did God keep His promise to Noah and his family? How do you think Noah and his family felt when they heard the rain and they were safe inside the boat?

Mini Muffin's Marvelous Muffins

"Mommi! Mommi!"

That was always a good way to get Mommi's attention. Especially when Mini Muffin ran up to Mommi, huffing and puffing when she said it.

"Tomorrow is our Sunday School teacher's birthday," said Mini. "Maria and I want to make a birthday cake for her."

"Oh, dear," said Mommi. "How about something a little easier for you to make?"

"Like what?" asked Mini.

"Like muffins," said Mommi. "Wouldn't it be fun for Mini Muffin to make muffins?"

"That would be fun!" Mini said, clapping her hands. "But would it be fun for you, Maria?"

Maria smiled and nodded her head, so Mommi got the muffin pans and the recipe book. "Now, would you like to make bran muffins, ginger muffins, oatmeal muffins, or peanut butter muffins?"

"Peanut butter!" said Mini.

"Ginger!" said Maria.

"Then you will each have to make your own kind," said Mommi. "Do you want me to help?"

"Maria and I want to do it," said Mini. "We'll call you if we need help. OK, Mommi?"

Mommi Muffin smiled. "I'll get everything out that you need," she said. "Then you may do it."

Mommi put the eggs, sugar, ginger, flour, salt, and other things on the counter. "Be sure to do exactly what the recipe says," Mommi called as she stepped into the other room.

Mini measured the peanut butter and mixed it with the sugar, just as the recipe said. Then she stirred in an egg and began to sift the baking powder and flour into it.

"Oh," Maria whispered softly to herself. "This ginger is good. But the recipe must be wrong. It says a teaspoon of ginger. If one teaspoon of ginger is good, think how marvelous it will be with six!"

Mini tried to do exactly what the recipe said. But Maria didn't.

"I don't like eggs," she thought. "That would spoil my muffins. And who wants that yukky flour in them?"

At last Mini and Maria put their muffins in some muffin pans and popped them in the oven to bake. Then they stood by the oven door and watched the clock.

At last the muffins were done. When they had cooled, Mini and Maria tasted Mini's peanut butter muffins first. "Ohhhh, they're marvelous!" said Maria. "Now let's try mine."

Maria took one bite of her ginger muffin. But she couldn't swallow it. Mini couldn't swallow her bite either. Maria tried to give the rest of her muffin to Ruff, but Ruff took one sniff and walked away.

"A dog won't even eat my muffins!" Maria cried.

When Mommi heard that, she came into the kitchen to see what was the matter. When Mommi tasted a ginger muffin she frowned. "It must have been a bad recipe, Maria," she said. "Which one did you follow?"

Maria hung her head. "I—I guess I really didn't follow the recipe," she said. "I thought my way was better. But now I have yukky ginger muffins."

"Then your yukky ginger muffins have done something very important for you today," said Mommi.

Maria looked surprised. "They have?" she asked. "What?"

"Maria," said Mommi, "why did Mini have marvelous muffins?"

Maria thought for a moment. "I suppose because she did what the recipe book said," she answered.

"Do you think you could have had marvelous muffins too?" Mommi asked.

Maria thought for two moments this time. "I suppose I could," she said, "if I had done what the recipe book said."

"Then the yukky ginger muffins taught you something important, didn't they?" Mommi asked.

"To do what the recipe book says," Maria added.

"Yes, but there's another book that's even more important to follow," said Mommi. "It's something like a recipe book, for it tells us how to make things come out right in our lives."

Maria smiled. "I know," she said. "The Bible."

"Right!" Mommi said. "When we do what God says in the Bible, things can become like marvelous muffins. But when we don't, they can become like yukky ginger muffins."

"I'll take the marvelous muffins!" Maria shouted.

"Me, too!" said Mini.

So everyone laughed as they tried just one more of Mini's marvelous muffins.

LET'S TALK ABOUT THIS

1. What did Mommi say about life becoming like yukky ginger muffins? Has that ever happened to you? What did you do about it?

2. How can we keep life from becoming like yukky ginger muffins? How did Noah do that? Why was it so important for Noah to do exactly what God said? Why is it so important for us?

The Tower Builders

GENESIS 11:1-9

"Nobody has ever done this before," the people said. "We'll be the greatest people in the world!"

It was true. Nobody had ever built such a tall tower before.

"We'll be famous!"

"Our tower will reach up into the sky!"

"No! Our tower will reach all the way up into heaven."

"That's it! A tower that reaches up to heaven. Who needs God? If we make a tall tower, we can just walk up!"

The people of Babel became more and more excited about their tower that would reach into heaven. They thought of their neighbors, admiring their tall tower and wishing they had one like it.

"Everyone will come to us," they said. "They will all come to use our tower."

God was not pleased with all of this. Nobody could walk up to His home in heaven on a tall tower. How foolish and proud these people were! They were even trying to take God's place by finding their own way to heaven.

"What will these foolish people try next if I let them do this?" God wondered. "They might do anything after this."

So God knew that He must stop this foolish tower. He must do something to keep the people from finishing it.

"I will give them different languages to speak," God said. "They will not understand what others say."

So God reached down among the people and gave them different languages. Then strange things began to happen.

32

One of the men shouted orders to another. He wanted to say, "Get those bricks up here!" But it sounded to the other man like "gobbley gobbley." So he didn't get the bricks up.

The other man began to shout other things. But everything he said sounded like "gobbley gobbley," too.

So the man with the bricks shouted back. He wanted to say, "Why don't you learn to talk?" But what he said really sounded like "booglie booglie."

Soon other men gathered around these two. They began to shout and argue. Some of them were "gobbleys" and some were "booglies."

Before long all the "gobbleys" became angry at the "booglies" and walked away from them. They threw down their bricks and left the tower.

"We will go somewhere else to live," they said. "We can't live with these strange people." Of course they still sounded like "gobbley gobbley" when they said this.

Then the "booglies" decided they would live together in another place, too. They certainly didn't want to be around people like the "gobbleys" either.

All around the tower the same thing happened to others, too. Before long, several little groups of people were leaving the tower to move away and live together in another place. These people did not know that God was using this to send them all over the world.

At last the tower stood alone. There were no more people to work on it. The wonderful tower that would reach to heaven would never be built. Some day it would crumble into the ground.

And all those proud people who tried to build their tower to heaven had lost many of their friends and neighbors. They had been too proud and their pride had hurt them.

WHAT DO YOU THINK?

1. How might this story have changed if these people had tried to reach heaven through God instead of their tower?
2. How can pride hurt people? How did it hurt the tower builders?
3. What happened to the tower builders? What does this tell us about different languages?

The Great Play House

"Where did you get all that junk, Maxi?" Poppi Muffin asked. Poppi had never seen so many old boards in anyone's back yard before! All he could do was stand there and shake his head.

"That's not junk," Maxi argued. "That happens to be the lumber for the greatest play house that has ever been built."

"Hmmmm," said Poppi. He often said hmmmm when he wasn't sure what else to say. It gave him a little time to think of something better. "And who is going to build this great play house?"

Maxi threw out his chest and tried to look important. "I am," he said. "I don't want anyone else to help me. I want to do this all by myself. Someone else will only mess it up."

"Hmmmm," said Poppi. But he couldn't think of anything else to say so he stopped with hmmmm this time. Maxi had said about all there was to say for now.

The next morning Mommi and Poppi woke up suddenly. There was a WHAM! BANG! WHAM! BANG! in the back yard. "Gracious!" said Mommi. "Whatever is that noise? It's so early the birds aren't up yet."

"Haven't you heard?" said Poppi. "That's the greatest play house in the world being built."

"You're going to help him build it, aren't you?" Mommi asked.

"I would only mess it up," said Poppi. "Maxi told me so."

That morning Maxi gulped his breakfast down and ran for the back door again. "Don't look until it's done!" he called back to Mommi and Poppi and Mini.

"Don't you want Poppi to help you, Maxi?" Mommi called.

"No," said Maxi. "This is going to be the greatest play house ever. I don't want anyone to mess it up."

"He really *did* say that," Mommi whispered to Poppi. She began to think about it so much that she sprinkled salt and pepper in her coffee and poured coffee cream on her eggs.

There was so much BANGING and WHAMMING in the back yard that Tuff crawled under the sofa to hide. Ruff sat in a corner of the living room and whined.

"Will the neighbors make us move away?" Mini asked.

Mommi smiled. "Not with the greatest play house in the world next door," she said.

It was almost time for lunch when Maxi ran into the kitchen. "IT'S DONE! IT'S DONE!" he shouted.

Maxi made so much noise that Ruff stopped whining and began to bark at him. Tuff ran from the sofa and hid in another room.

"NOW you can all come out to see it," said Maxi.

But when Mommi and Poppi looked at the play house they hardly knew what to say.

'Hmmmm," said Poppi.

"Gracious!" said Mommi.

"It's ugly," said Mini.

"It is NOT," shouted Maxi. He was so angry that he went inside and slammed the door behind him.

But when the door slammed, the great play house began to wobble. Then it shook and fell down into a pile of old boards with Maxi under the pile.

Mommi and Poppi ran to the pile of boards and began pulling them from Maxi. "Maxi! Are you hurt?" Mommi cried out.

Maxi poked his head up from the boards. "No, but my great play house is a mess," he said. "I—I guess I needed a little help after all."

Mommi smiled at Maxi. "Some things Maxis do best, and some things Poppis do best," she said. "And some things Maxis do best when Poppis help them."

"Hmmmm," said Poppi. "I think you're right. So what if I help you build a play house from these boards? It may not be the greatest play house in the world, but it will be fun."

Maxi was happy to hear this. And he didn't say a word about someone else messing it up.

LET'S TALK ABOUT THIS

1. What did Mommi say about the things that Maxis and Poppis do best? What do you think about that?

2. How was Maxi like the tower builders at first? What caused him to change?

3. Do you do some things best when God helps you? What would you like Him to help you do now? Will you ask Him?

CHILDREN JESUS KNEW

Stop Crying!

LUKE 7:11-17

"Where are we going?" a disciple asked.

"Who knows?" said another. "Ask Jesus."

But the disciple didn't ask Jesus. He was happy to go anywhere with Jesus.

The disciples followed Jesus past olive trees and fields of wheat. Up hills and through valleys they went. At last they came to a little village.

"Why are we going to Nain?" the disciple asked.

"Who knows?" said the other. "Ask Jesus."

But the disciple didn't have time to ask Jesus. Just then some people came through the gate of the village. They walked slowly.

42

Some of the people were crying. All of them looked sad.

"It's a funeral!" whispered a disciple.

"That poor woman's son has died," said another. "What will she do now?"

It was true. The poor woman's son had died. Now she and her friends were taking him outside the village to bury him. Then she would be alone, for she had no one else to care for her.

"If only Jesus could have come before," whispered a disciple. "Perhaps He could have healed the boy. Then he would not have died."

The people of Nain came closer and closer. When they came near Jesus, they stopped. Everyone became quiet now, for they were all waiting for Jesus to say something.

"Don't cry!" Jesus said.

The people began to look at one another. How could Jesus say that? Couldn't He see that this was a funeral? Didn't He know that this young man was all that his mother had?

Then Jesus walked over to the young man's body. People began to whisper softly to one another.

"What will He say?"

"What will He do?"

Slowly Jesus stretched out His hand and touched the young man's body. No one whispered now. Only the wind whispered as it gently tugged at the white cloth that covered the young man.

"Come back to life!" Jesus said softly.

People began to whisper to one another again. "Nobody can come back to life when they are dead," they said. "Doesn't Jesus know that?"

Everyone became quiet again as the white cloth began to move. They could hardly believe their eyes as the young man sat up and smiled.

"Look!" the people shouted. "He's alive again! Look what Jesus has done!"

Everyone began to talk at once. But the young man and his mother didn't hear a word they said. They were too happy to listen.

WHAT DO YOU THINK?

1. Who can bring someone back to life again? Can anyone today bring a person back from the dead?
2. Why could Jesus do this? Who is He?
3. If Jesus can do anything, why don't we ask Him to help us more often? Will you?

If I Could Do Anything

"Now you be careful today, Ruff," said Mini. "Don't go off and follow those bunny tracks like you usually do."

Ruff and Tuff were excited whenever Maxi and Mini went for a hike in the woods. Tuff liked to chase dry leaves that blew across the path or play with vines that hung down from the trees.

But Ruff had only one thing in mind on a hike. He would find a fresh bunny track, then follow it as fast as he could. Ruff never did catch a bunny. But it was fun to try. In a few minutes he would come back huffing and puffing.

Maxi and Mini had just set the lunch basket down when Ruff began barking. "Yiiik, yiiik, yiiik," he cried as he took off on a fast run through the woods.

"Oh, no," said Mini. "Not at lunch time. Ruff, come back here!"

But Ruff was too far away to hear Mini. All Mini could hear now was a small "yiiik, yiiik," as Ruff followed the bunny trail.

"Let's eat," said Maxi. "That dumb bunny chaser will find his way back when he's tired."

"But what if he doesn't?" asked Mini. "What if he loses his way and gets lost?"

Maxi shrugged his shoulders and spread out the potato chips and peanut butter sandwiches. After Maxi and Mini thanked God for the food, they began to eat.

Mini spoiled the lunch by asking about Ruff every few minutes. "Why don't you forget that dumb mutt," Maxi growled each time.

But Maxi started to worry by the time lunch was over. Ruff had never been gone this long before. They couldn't hear a sound from him either.

"What will we do?" asked Mini. "I'm afraid he's lost. How will we find him?"

"I know," said Maxi. "I'll grow some big wings like a bird and fly over the woods. Then I can see everything."

Mini laughed. "Silly," she said. "Let's see you."

"All right, here I go," shouted Maxi. He stood up and flapped his arms. Tuff let out a meow and ran behind a stump.

Maxi imagined that he was flying over the woods. But just when he was almost to the clouds, Mini stopped his daydream. "It's fun to pretend, Maxi, but Ruff is lost. We've got to find him."

"OK, I'll take one of these super-duper space tablets, and I can be anywhere I want," said Maxi. He popped a leftover potato chip into his mouth and chewed. Then he gave one to Mini.

"You'd better take one, too," he said. "I don't want to leave you behind."

Mini quickly chewed a potato chip while Maxi pressed the button on his sleeve. "Ready? Here we go!" Maxi called out. "We're going to the far edge of the woods. I see it! There's Ruff and Big Bunny, having a cup of tea at a table for two."

"MAXI!" Mini shouted. Maxi woke up from his daydream.

"This is fun, Maxi," said Mini. "But it really isn't helping us find Ruff."

"You're right," said Maxi. "I wish I could go anywhere and do anything. Then we could find Ruff. But nobody can do that."

Mini thought for a moment. "I know someone who can," she said.

Maxi looked surprised. "Who?" he asked.

"Jesus!" said Mini. "We should ask Him to help us. He knows where Ruff is."

Maxi and Mini closed their eyes and began to talk to Jesus. But while they did, Maxi felt something cold on his nose.

"Don't bother me now, Ruff," said Maxi. "We're asking Jesus to help us find—"

Maxi didn't finish. Two pairs of arms reached out and hugged a huffy, puffy dog.

Poor Ruff wondered why, too. He hadn't even caught the bunny!

LET'S TALK ABOUT THIS
1. What can Jesus do? Where can He go? Can He do anything? What did the widow at Nain learn about Jesus?
2. What did Maxi and Mini say about Jesus? If Jesus can do anything, why don't you ask Him to help you more often? Will you?

Too Late Is Never Too Late

LUKE 8:41-42,49-56

"Please help my daughter," Jairus begged. "She is so sick. I'm afraid that she is dying."

Jesus put His hand on Jairus' arm. Then He smiled. Somehow Jairus felt that things would work out right now. Jesus could heal his daughter. He was sure of that.

He had seen Jesus heal others many times. So why wouldn't He do that for Jairus, the leader of the synagogue in Jesus' home town? Wasn't he one of the most important men in Capernaum?

But Jairus grew nervous as they pushed their way through the crowds. They could hardly walk! Then a woman came along who needed help and Jesus stopped to help her, too.

"Please come!" Jairus begged. "I'm afraid we may be too late."

When Jairus said that, a friend pushed through the crowds to meet him. "You are too late!" the friend whispered sadly. "Your daughter is dead."

Jairus put his face in his hands and almost cried. If only Jesus had not stopped to help that woman. Perhaps He could have reached Jairus' daughter in time to heal her.

Then he felt Jesus' hand touch him again. "Don't worry," Jesus said softly. "Please trust Me."

48

When Jesus came into Jairus' home, He heard loud noises. People were not sitting quietly around the girl. They were moaning and groaning and crying. They were making so much noise that Jesus felt sad for them.

"Why are you moaning and groaning like that?" Jesus asked. "Don't you know that Jairus' girl is just sleeping? She isn't dead."

The moaners and groaners stopped making their noises. They looked at Jesus. Then they began to laugh. They began to make fun of Him. Anyone could see that the girl was dead!

"Get out of here!" Jesus told the moaners and groaners. "I have work to do."

Then Jesus went with Jairus and his wife to see the girl. When Jairus saw his daughter lying there so still he knew that she was dead. Why did Jesus say that she was sleeping?

Then Jesus took the girl's hand in His and spoke to her. "Get up, little girl!" He said tenderly.

Slowly her eyes fluttered and opened. Then she saw her father and mother and reached her arms toward them and smiled.

"Give her some food," Jesus suggested. "And please don't tell what happened here."

Jairus and his wife were so happy that they would do anything Jesus asked. Now Jairus was sure that it was never too late to ask Jesus to help.

WHAT DO YOU THINK?

1. Why did Jairus think at first that he might be too late for Jesus to help? What changed his mind?
2. Do you think it is ever too late to ask Jesus for help? Why not?

That Dumb Cat

"Tuff Muffin! You get down from that pole!"

But no matter how much Mini Muffin shouted at Tuff, she would only sit on top of the electric pole and meow. Of course, there was no way for Mini to climb the pole either.

"That dumb cat," said Mini. "Why did she ever climb up the pole when that ugly, old dog chased her? Why didn't she run under a bush or something?"

Mini Muffin called and called. She begged and yelled and called some more. But Tuff was afraid to climb down the pole.

Suddenly Mini heard a loud rumbling BOOM A ROOM A BOOM. Then she looked behind her and saw that the sky was dark with flashes of lightning. She heard the thunder rumble again.

"Oh no," Mini cried out. "What will I do? Tuff will drown up there in a storm, or the lightning will hit her."

Mini ran for home as fast as her legs would take her. There was Poppi, rushing out to the patio to take the cushions of the chairs inside before the storm came.

"Poppi! Poppi!" Mini shouted. "Come quick. Tuff is on top of an electric pole and a big storm is coming and she's going to drown or get struck with lightning and—"

"Whoa, wait a minute," said Poppi. "I've got to get these cushions in before it rains or they will get soaked."

"But we'll be too late," Mini cried out.

"Can't help it, Mini," said Poppi. "How about giving me a little help?"

Mini grew more frantic with every passing second. The storm was coming closer and closer. "Who cares about these old cushions," she thought. "Tuff is more important to me."

52

At last the cushions were in. "Now what did you say about Tuff?" Poppi asked.

"She's up on an electric pole and the storm is coming and she's going to get struck with lightning or drown or something," Mini said without catching a breath.

"Mini, you know I can't climb an electric pole with a storm coming," said Poppi. "And we'd never get the fire department here before that storm comes."

"Then what can we DO?" Mini asked frantically.

"Well, we can pray as we run over there and see Tuff," said Poppi. "Maybe we can coax her down or something."

Mini tried to pray and say "that dumb cat" at the same time. But it didn't seem to mix too well. She did manage to pray a little in the minute or two that it took to run to the pole. But she was sure that they were too late to help Tuff.

"Look!" said Poppi. "There's a big fire truck by the pole."

"And Tuff is gone," Mini wailed. "She's probably dead or something. Maybe they ran over her."

"On top of an electric pole?" asked Poppi.

But Mini changed from tears to smiles as a fireman walked around the big truck. "Is this your cat?" he asked. "I saw it on the pole as we were going home. Thought we'd better get it down before that storm gets here."

Mini wasn't sure which to squeeze harder, Tuff or the fireman. But there wasn't much time to do either, for the first big drops of rain were beginning to fall as everyone ran for home.

"Thank You, Lord," Mini prayed as they ran. "Thank you that even too late is never too late for You."

LET'S TALK ABOUT THIS

1. Is it ever too late for the Lord to help us? Would you have thought so if you had been Mini at first?

2. What would you have thought if you had seen the fireman holding your pet cat? What would you have said to the Lord?

The Man Who Is Never Too Busy

MARK 10:13-16

"You can't bring those children here!" the disciples told some mothers and fathers. "Don't you see how busy Jesus is?"

The mothers and fathers certainly did see how busy Jesus was. People were crowding around Him on every side. The blind wanted to see. The crippled wanted to walk. The sick wanted to be healed. They were all begging Jesus to help them. It didn't seem like a very good time for children to come too.

"Go away," the disciples said. "Jesus is very, very busy."

But the children would not go away. The mothers and fathers would not go away either.

"We want to see Jesus," said the children.

"And we want Jesus to see them," said the mothers and fathers.

Everyone was talking so loud now that Jesus came over to see what was going on. "What is the matter?" He asked.

"These people have brought their children to see You," said the disciples. "But we told them to go away. You are too busy to bother with them."

Jesus smiled as He looked at the children. He knew how much they wanted to see Him.

"Let the children come to Me," said Jesus. "You must not send them away, for anyone who wants to go to heaven must first become like one of them."

The disciples hardly knew what to say. What was Jesus telling them? Then they knew that these little children believed in Jesus with all their hearts. Many of the people in the crowd did not believe. Their hearts were still hard and cold. No wonder Jesus said that they must become like the little children.

So the crowd waited while Jesus talked with the children. For a while, the sick would not be healed, the crippled would not walk, and the blind would not see, not until Jesus had talked with His special friends, the children. For a while, everything else would wait.

"Look at that," someone whispered. "Jesus isn't too busy for the children now, is He?"

"No," said another. "I don't think He will ever be too busy for them!"

WHAT DO YOU THINK?

1. Why did the disciples tell the mothers and fathers not to bother Jesus? Why did He seem to be too busy?
2. What did Jesus say about the children? Did He think He was too busy to see them? How do you know?
3. Do you think Jesus is too busy to listen to you? Why not?

The Newspaper

"Poppi!"

"Uh huh."

"Poppi. Do you love me?"

"Uh huh."

"Poppi. Would you do something special for me?"

"Uh huh."

Poppi was reading his newspaper. And when Poppi was doing that, he really was too busy for anything. Even for Mini Muffin.

"Poppi."

"Uh huh."

"Poppi. Would you still love me if I brought a friend home?"

"Uh huh."

"But he's a big friend with a lot of hair. Is that OK?"

"Uh huh."

"And he barks and has to be fed. You'll let me bring him here, won't you?"

"Uh huh."

"Oh, Poppi, that's wonderful. He's so lonely. Someone has dumped him out and he has no place to go. May I keep him?"

"Uh huh."

"Thank you, Poppi. Thank you. I'll go get him right now. Is it OK to bring him here in the living room?"

"Uh huh."

"OK, Poppi. You wait right here and I'll go get him. We'll be back soon. You'll stay here until we get back won't you?"

"Uh huh."

Mini Muffin ran from the house as fast as she could go. Down the street she ran to find her big, hairy friend.

"There you are, Buster," Mini said at last. "You're coming home with me. You can be Ruff's big brother."

Buster tagged along behind Mini. He followed her into the house and through the living room to Poppi. Poppi was still reading his newspaper.

"Poppi."

"Uh huh."

"My friend Buster is here. You said he could stay with us, didn't you?"

"Uh huh."

"Buster, go meet Poppi and give him a big love."

Suddenly Buster poked his head up under Poppi's newspaper and touched his cold nose to Poppi's nose.

"YEOOOWWWW!" Poppi shouted, jumping from his chair. "Get that monster out of here! He's attacking me."

But Buster just stood there, wagging his tail.

"You told me I could bring him here, Poppi," said Mini. Then Mini told Poppi all that he had said.

Poppi hung his head. "I'm sorry, Mini. I was just too busy with my newspaper. I didn't hear a word you said. But I'll help you find the right home for Buster."

So Poppi and Mini went out to find a new home for Buster. And Poppi was sure that he would not be too busy again. After all, what might Mini Muffin bring home next?

LET'S TALK ABOUT THIS

1. In what way was Poppi too busy for Mini? How did this get the Muffins into a problem?

2. In the Bible story, how was Jesus different from Poppi? Is Jesus ever too busy for us? Which problems should we not take to Him? Are there any?

3. If you know that Jesus is never too busy, what should you do the next time you have a problem?

If You Want to Be First

MATTHEW 18:1-10

"I wonder which one of us will be the most important in Jesus' kingdom?" a disciple asked.

It was too bad he asked that, for it started a big argument. Everyone thought that he would be more important than the others.

"I carry the money!" said Judas. "The man with the money is always on top!"

"But we're Jesus' closest friends," said Peter, James, and John. "Jesus would always put His best friends first."

"What about me?" Matthew may have asked. "Aren't you forgetting that I was a Roman tax collector? Not one of you ever held an important job like that!"

So they argued and fussed all the way home. Sometimes they argued so loud that they were sure that Jesus may have heard them. They hoped that He didn't, for they would be ashamed for Him to know about this silly argument.

Before long, they stopped to rest along the way. A little boy played near their resting place.

"You're about as important as that little boy!" one of the disciples grumbled to another. That was his way of saying that his friend wasn't very important at all.

The other disciple didn't have time to give an answer. Jesus sat down with them and he certainly didn't want Jesus to hear their argument.

"What have you been talking about?" Jesus asked the disciples.

The disciples looked at each other. Then they looked down at the ground. What could they say? At last someone had the courage to speak.

"Which of us will be the most important in Your kingdom?" he asked.

All eyes looked at Jesus. Which one would He say? Would it be Matthew? Or Judas? Or would it be Jesus' closest friends, Peter, James, or John?

Jesus walked quietly to the little boy playing nearby. He took the little boy's hand and led him back to the disciples. The disciples were sure that Jesus would tell them how they shouldn't be like that little boy if they wanted to be the greatest. They must be big, and powerful, and important.

"Anyone who becomes like this little boy will be the greatest in My kingdom," Jesus said quietly.

The disciples could hardly believe their ears. What did this little boy have that was great?

He wasn't big and strong.

He wasn't wise or powerful.

He didn't have a big job as Matthew had.

He didn't have money as Judas had.

And he wasn't doing big things all day, just playing.

But the little boy wasn't proud, either. And he wasn't arguing about being the greatest.

"Whoever gives up all his pride and comes to Me like a little child will be the greatest," Jesus said. "You must turn away from your sin and turn to God if you want to be part of My kingdom."

The disciples were ashamed. They were trying to be first, the most important. Now Jesus was telling them to put God first and themselves last. That is the way to be great in Jesus' kingdom.

There wasn't one more argument all day about being first!

WHAT DO YOU THINK?

1. Why did the disciples want to be first, or the greatest, in Jesus' kingdom? Do most people want to be first?
2. How did the disciples think they could become the greatest? How do most people think they can become the greatest, or first?
3. But how did Jesus say that people become the greatest in His kingdom?

I'm First

"I'm first!" Maxi shouted.

"No, I'm first!" said Mini.

"Poppi, I was first," they both said.

Poppi frowned. "What seems to be the problem?" he asked.

"Mommi made some lemonade, and Maxi ran through the door and got his glass first," Mini complained.

"But I *was* first," Maxi snapped back.

"Hmmmm," said Poppi, "Too bad you didn't get your lemonade, Maxi."

"Oh, but I did," said Maxi as he took a sip. "It's just that I was first."

"Then you didn't get your lemonade, Mini?" Poppi asked with a frown.

"I got my lemonade," said Mini, holding up her glass. "It's good, too. But I was first, that's all."

Poppi shook his head and went out to work in the garage. About the time Maxi and Mini were finishing their lemonade, Poppi came back through the door.

"OK, now, who'll be first?" he shouted.

"I will!" Maxi snapped before Mini could swallow the lemonade in her mouth.

"That's not fair," Mini complained. "I couldn't say anything with all that lemonade in my mouth."

"Sorry, Mini, but Maxi is first," said Poppi. Then Poppi reached behind the door and brought out a push broom.

"Be my guest!" said Poppi. "I need someone to help me sweep the garage."

Maxi looked as if he had eaten a jar of lemons. But what can you do when you say you're first? So Maxi went out with the broom while Mini giggled.

Poppi told Mommi all about "I'm first" while Mini and Maxi were washing for dinner. That gave Mommi a good idea. When dinner was almost over, Mommi waited until Maxi had taken a big bite of chicken.

"OK, who'll be first?" she called out across the table.

Maxi tried to say "I will" but all he could say was "mm ffg." So Mini won that time.

"I will!" she sang out.

"Good," said Mommi. "I need someone to help me dry the dishes tonight."

Mini frowned and put her chin on her hands. Maxi tried to laugh but it was too hard with a mouthful of chicken.

Everyone was very quiet until it was time for dessert. Then Poppi suddenly shouted out, "OK, who'll be first?"

Maxi and Mini both started to say "I will," but they stopped and looked at each other. "Let Maxi be first," said Mini.

"No, I think Mini should be first," said Maxi.

"That sounds much better," said Poppi, "but I have a better idea. Let's ask Mommi to be first this time."

Then Poppi whispered something in Mini's and Maxi's ears and the three of them hurried into the kitchen with the dirty dishes. "Stay there!" said Poppi. "This is a secret."

In a few minutes, Poppi and Maxi and Mini all came back with Mommi's dessert. "You're first," they said.

"That was fun," said Maxi and Mini. "It really is more fun putting someone else first."

"That's what Jesus told us," said Poppi. "We'll read about that now in The Muffin Family Picture Bible." So they did.

LET'S TALK ABOUT THIS
1. How did Jesus say that people could be first, or greatest, in heaven?
2. What did Maxi and Mini learn about being first? Did they find it was more fun to put themselves first or others?
3. Who have you been putting first in your family? Yourself? Others? What did you learn from the Bible story and the Muffin Family story?
4. What will you do this week to put others first? What do you think God will think of that? How will you feel about it?

THE ORPHAN QUEEN

The Orphan Queen

ESTHER 2:1-20

"How can I find a queen to rule the land with me?" the king asked.

The king's helpers thought about this. It was not easy to find a queen. She must be a very special person who would please the king. And she must be very beautiful, too.

"We have an idea," they said at last. "We will have some men look for the most beautiful girls in all the land. Then we will bring them here so that you may meet them. The girl who pleases you most will be your queen."

The king liked this very much. Before long, messengers went everywhere, looking for the most beautiful girls in the land. Then they returned to the palace from far and near with girls who wanted to become the queen.

For a year each girl lived in a special part of the palace, learning to dress like a queen and learning to use sweet perfumes. Then she went to see the king.

One day it was Esther's turn to see the king. She dressed in the finest clothes and put on her best perfume. Esther was so beautiful and such a wonderful person that all the other girls were sure that she would be the new queen.

But Esther was not sure. She was only a poor orphan girl who lived with her Uncle Mordecai. Not only that, she was a Jewish girl. Her people had been captured and brought to this land years before.

"You must not tell anyone that you are a Jewish girl," her uncle had warned. "The king may not want a foreign girl for his queen."

But nobody at the palace asked if she was a foreign girl. Nobody seemed to care. Esther was such a beautiful, kind, and loving person that everyone seemed to love her, no matter what she was.

The king loved Esther so much that he put a crown upon her head and chose her to be his queen. Esther was sure that she had pleased her king most because she had tried to please God most, too.

The king gave a big party and gave many good gifts to show everyone how happy he was with his new queen. Of course, Queen Esther was happy, too. She had tried to please God in all that she had done. So Esther knew that God had helped her become queen.

"Thank You, Lord," she must have prayed many times. "Thank You for helping me become the queen of our great land."

WHAT DO YOU THINK?

1. Do you think you would have liked Queen Esther? Why? Why do you think others liked her?

2. What helped Esther most to become queen? Whom did Esther try to please?

3. How might the story have changed if Esther had not pleased the king? How might it have changed if she had not pleased God?

Tuff Luck

Mini thought it was so much fun to watch Grand-mommi knit. She liked to stand by Grandmommi's chair and watch her knitting needles fly back and forth.

"You knit so fast, Grandmommi," said Mini. "And you make such pretty things from an old ball of yarn."

"Thank you, Mini," said Grandmommi as she pulled the ball of yarn closer to her chair. Grand-mommi looked over her glasses to see how much yarn was on the ball, then went back to her knitting.

"What are you making this time?" Mini asked.

Grandmommi smiled. "Does this look like a scarf for your father?"

Mini wasn't sure what it looked like so she shrugged her shoulders. Then she and Grandmommi talked about knitting and all the things that Grand-mommi had made.

Before long, Grandmommi stopped knitting and looked over her glasses again to see how much yarn was on the ball. But when she did, her mouth fell open.

"It's gone!" she shouted. "My ball of yarn is gone!"

Sure enough, the ball was gone. Instead, there was a long piece of yarn that went all the way from Grandmommi to the door and beyond.

"Something is fishy here," Grandmommi said as she stood up to look at the yarn. "Seems to me there's a yarn thief in this house. Let's follow this yarn quietly and see where it goes."

Grandmommi and Mini slipped quietly along the yarn. They went through the living room door into the dining room. They followed it through two more doors into Grandmommi's bedroom.

"Ahah!" Grandmommi said as they came into her bedroom.

There at the end of the yarn sat Tuff, playing with the little tiny ball that was left. But when Tuff heard Grandmommi say "Ahah" she jumped up and arched her back.

"Yeoww," said Tuff, almost spitting it back.

"Don't you yeoww at me, you yarn stealer," said Grandmommi. "That's a no no."

"But Grandmommi," said Mini. "Tuff was just having fun."

"I know, Mini," Grandmommi answered. "But it won't be fun for me to roll all that yarn up again. I know that Tuff didn't realize that she was hurting me, so we'll forgive her. But fun is not fun when it pleases us and hurts others."

Mini thought about that for a minute. "Is that just as true if we please ourselves and hurt God?" she asked.

"Yes, Mini," said Grandmommi. "But much more so."

Mini thought for another minute. "Grandmommi, may I roll up the yarn for you?" she asked.

Grandmommi smiled a big Grandmommi type smile. "That would be sweet of you, Mini," she said. "What gave you that idea?"

"Well, I figure if I can please my Grandmommi who loves God, then that will also please God," said Mini.

"Bless your heart," said Grandmommi. "Then I know it will please you, too."

Then Mini looked at Tuff sitting in the corner of the bedroom. "Poor Tuff," she said. "Now she won't have a ball of yarn to play with."

"Tuff luck!" said Grandmommi. "But I have another ball she can play with."

So Tuff played with the ball while Mini rolled the yarn back to Grandmommi, who was knitting again in her chair. It almost seemed that everyone was happy!

LET'S TALK ABOUT THIS
1. How did Mini try to please God? Who else did she please?
2. How was Mini like Queen Esther? How would things have been different if Mini had gone out to play and let Grandmommi roll up the yarn? Would that have pleased Mini as much as helping Grandmommi? Why not?
3. Think of some ways you can please God by pleasing others this week. Then try to do at least one of them.

Sealed with the King's Ring

ESTHER 3

"Why don't you obey the king?" some people asked Mordecai. "Why don't you bow down before Haman?"

Mordecai shook his head. "Haman is a very bad man," he said. "I must please God. God would not be pleased if I bowed before Haman, even though the king did make him an important man."

Some of the people told Haman what Mordecai had said. Haman was very angry when he heard this. Hadn't the king made Haman ruler of the land? Only the king was greater than he was. How dare Mordecai refuse to bow before him!

"So, this Jew will not bow before me," Haman growled. "I will have every Jew in the land killed. We will see if that will please their God!"

Before long, Haman went to see the king. "There are some people in our land who refuse to obey you," Haman lied. "They are different from us. They ought to be killed. I will even put some of my money into the royal treasury to do this."

The king thought that Haman was a good man. If Haman said that these people should not live, he would let him kill them.

So the king took a ring from his finger. The ring had some small pictures on it. Whenever people saw these pictures on something, they knew that the king had stamped his ring on it. They knew that they must do whatever the letter told them to do, for the king had signed it with his ring.

"Take my ring," the king told Haman. "Write some letters and sign them with my ring. Then you may send these letters over all the land."

Haman smiled as he walked from the palace with the king's ring. He smiled even more as he walked past Mordecai, sitting near the palace gate.

"It won't be long now, Mordecai," Haman whispered to himself. "You and your people will soon die!"

A few days later, Haman wrote some letters. "On the chosen day, you will kill all Jews who live near you," the letter said. "When you do, you may keep everything these Jews have."

Then Haman sent messengers all over the land with the letters. "The king orders you to obey this law!" Haman said to the people.

Haman was so happy that he went to see the king again. He wanted to tell the king that he had sent the letters, ordering all Jews to be killed.

But the king did not know that something strange was about to happen. He did not know that God would take care of these people who tried to please Him most.

WHAT DO YOU THINK?

1. Why did Haman get so angry at Mordecai? What had Mordecai done?

2. Why did Mordecai refuse to bow before Haman? Would God have been pleased if he had?

3. Could Mordecai please both God and Haman? Which did he choose to please?

82

Better than a Best Friend

"Maxi, you've got to help me!"

Pookie talked like he really needed help, too. At least, Maxi thought he did.

"What's the matter, Pookie?" Maxi asked. "Got your chewing gum in your hair or something?"

"Funny, funny," Pookie growled. "It's no time to be cute. I really need you. You're my best friend, aren't you? Huh, Maxi, aren't you?"

"Sure, Pookie, what do you need?" Maxi asked.

Pookie hung his head. "Come on downtown with me while I tell you," he said.

So Pookie told Maxi about his problem as they walked downtown. "You know where they're building the new apartments?" Pookie asked. "Well, my dad told me to stay away from there so I won't get hurt."

"And you didn't?" Maxi asked.

"Yeah, I was over there this morning," Pookie admitted, holding his head down. "I was bouncing the new ball that my dad got at Tucker's Toy Shop and it bounced into a cement mixer."

By this time, Pookie and Maxi were standing outside Tucker's Toy Shop. "Maxi, I want you to go in and ask Mr. Tucker to show you some model planes," said Pookie. "While he's doing that, I'll pick up a ball just like the one I lost and walk out. Then you can come out in a couple of minutes. He'll never know what happened."

"Sorry Pookie," said Maxi. "I won't help you steal something."

"Hey, wait, I'm not stealing. I'm just taking it," Pookie argued. "Anyway, you're my best friend. Remember?"

"Sure Pookie, but *my* Best Friend wouldn't like that and I want to please Him more than you," Maxi answered.

"Who's that?"

"Jesus."

"OK. But you've just got to do something else for me," said Pookie.

About this time, Pookie and Maxi passed Pop's Sweet Shop. There was Chief Carter, eating an ice cream sundae. "Hi, boys!" said the chief.

Pookie gulped nervously as he said "hi" and hurried on with Maxi. It was the wrong time to see the chief of police.

"What do you want me to do now?" asked Maxi.

"Come home with me and tell my folks I was at your house this morning," said Pookie.

"Sorry, Pookie," said Maxi. "I won't tell a lie to help you."

"But that's not lying," said Pookie. "It's just—well, it's sorta telling something that isn't quite true."

"No way, Pookie," said Maxi. "My Best Friend wouldn't like that and I want to please Him more than you."

"I know, I know," said Pookie. "You want to please Jesus more than me. Right?"

"Right, Pookie," said Maxi. "Anything else I can do for you?"

"Sure, Maxi," said Pookie. "Come home with me while I tell my dad that I'm sorry. A best friend can do that, can't he?"

Maxi smiled. "A best friend would be glad to be a best friend when you want to do that!" he said.

So the best friends headed toward Pookie's house. Maxi decided that he would ask his really truly Best Friend to help his other best friend say the best thing.

LET'S TALK ABOUT THIS

1. Why is it important to please Jesus more than our best friends? In the Bible story, who did Mordecai please?

2. What are some things that please Jesus? What can you do to please Jesus most? Will you do some of these things today?

A Brave Queen Who Saved Her People

ESTHER 4—9

"Why are you dressed in that old cloth, Mordecai?" some of his friends asked. "And why are you wailing and crying out here in the streets?"

Mordecai had torn his clothes, put ashes on his face, and gone out in the streets to moan and cry. "Haven't you heard what Haman did?" he asked. "Haven't you heard that he has ordered all our people killed?"

When Queen Esther found that Mordecai was dressed the way he was and was wailing and crying in the streets, she sent a messenger to find out why. "Haman is going to kill all the Jews," said Mordecai. "He will even kill you there in the palace. You must beg the king to save our lives."

Queen Esther was afraid. She did not dare to see the king unless he asked her to come. That was the law. The king could kill anyone who did that.

"You must go!" Mordecai told her. "If you don't you may die anyway. God may have made you queen so that you can save His people."

So Queen Esther went to see the king. Slowly she walked into the big room where the king sat upon his throne. Everyone looked at the beautiful queen. Then the king looked at her. What would he do?

Then the king held out his golden scepter. That meant that he was willing to talk with Esther and would not hurt her. Esther knew now that the king loved her very much. Perhaps he would help her change Haman's wicked orders. Esther's people were all praying that he would, so perhaps God could use her to save them.

"What may I do for you?" the king asked. "What may I give you?"

"Come to my dinner," said Esther. "Tell Haman to come, too, for I have prepared a lovely dinner for both of you."

The king and Haman were happy to come to Queen Esther's dinner. They were happy to be with their beautiful queen. The only thing Haman wanted more was to have Mordecai bow down before him.

"What do you really want?" the king asked at the dinner. "I will give you anything."

"Come to another dinner tomorrow," said the queen. "I will tell you then what I really want."

Haman was so happy when he went home. He told his wife what an important man he was. "The king and I are the only ones invited to the queen's dinner," he said.

The next day the king's men came to take Haman to the queen's dinner. Haman was very proud as he went in. Who in all the land was as important as he? Only the king was greater. Why shouldn't Mordecai bow down before him? He was glad now that he had ordered the Jews killed. That would show people how important he was. And Mordecai would be killed, for he was a Jew.

"What do you want, Queen Esther?" the king asked again when they were eating. "I will give you anything."

"Anything?" the queen asked. "Then save my life and the lives of my people. Some evil man has made plans to kill us."

The king was angry when he heard that. "Who would dare do such a wicked thing?" he roared.

Then Queen Esther looked at Haman. "This wicked man!" she shouted. "He has ordered me and all my people killed."

The king was so angry that he hurried from the room to think. Haman began to tremble. He had not known that the queen was a Jew. So Haman fell down on his knees and begged Queen Esther to save his life. When the king came back into the room, he was even more angry to see Haman with his queen.

Then one of the king's helpers had an idea. "Did you know that Haman made a gallows to hang Queen Esther's uncle, Mordecai?" he asked. "Haman wanted to kill Mordecai because he would not bow down before him."

"Then we will hang Haman on his own gallows!" the king shouted.

The king gave Haman's job to Mordecai. He gave Haman's property to Queen Esther.

"If you love me, change Haman's wicked law!" Queen Esther begged.

So the king let Queen Esther and Mordecai make a new law. The new law kept people from killing Queen Esther's people.

Queen Esther's people were so happy that she had saved their lives. She had been very brave to ask the king for help.

"Thank You, Lord, for Queen Esther," they must have prayed.

WHAT DO YOU THINK?

1. How do you know that Queen Esther was brave? What could have happened to her when she went to see the king?

2. How would you have felt about Queen Esther if you had been one of her people? How do you feel about her now?

3. In what ways could you be like Queen Esther? In what ways would you want to be like her?

A Very Wet Walk

Mini and Maria were both sopping wet.

"You dumb Donald Doolittle," Mini shouted. "That's the second time you've done that to us."

"What are we going to do?" Maria asked. "Every time he hears us go by this board fence, he's going to throw a bucket of water on us."

"Oh no he isn't," said Mini. "I'm going to stop him right now!"

"But Mini," Maria argued. "Aren't you afraid he might do something worse if you do?"

"I'm not afraid," said Mini.

Mini marched right up to the Doolittle door and rang the bell. Before long, the door opened and there stood Mrs. Doolittle.

"Mini, let's go home," whispered Maria. "I'm scared." But Mini stood there, looking very wet and a little angry.

"Gracious, whatever happened to you girls?" asked Mrs. Doolittle. "You're all wet! Can I help you with something?"

"Yes, you can," said Mini. "Please walk to the corner with us."

"But why?" asked Mrs. Doolittle.

"I'll tell you when we get there," said Mini. "But please don't say a word until we're there. Just let Maria and me talk."

Mrs. Doolittle looked puzzled as she walked beside the board fence with Mini and Maria. They were talking and laughing but they didn't want her to say a word.

Suddenly Mrs. Doolittle cried out. "Ooh! I'm soaking wet! Where did that come from?"

Just then a face peeked over the fence, looking straight into the face of Mrs. Doolittle. It was Donald.

"So that's it," said Mrs. Doolittle. "You get over here this instant, Donald Doolittle, and apologize to these girls."

Mini wanted to call him dumb Donald when he stood there, apologizing. But she didn't. She almost felt sorry for him.

"Thank you for taking a walk with us, Mrs. Doolittle," Mini said as she turned to leave.

"That was a very brave thing to do, Mini," said Maria. "I was afraid."

"So is Donald about now," said Mini. Then both girls laughed and went home to change.

LET'S TALK ABOUT THIS

1. Is it better to run away from problems or to face them? Which did Mini do? How did she face her problem?
2. How was Mini like Queen Esther? What would you have done if you were Mini?
3. Think of some problems you have now. How can you face them instead of running away? How can you get help from God?

COURAGE
WITH KINGS AND SHIPWRECKS

Telling Someone About a Friend

ACTS 25:13—26:32

"What has he done?" King Agrippa asked.

"Nothing!" said Governor Festus. "I don't see why those people want to kill Paul. But I want you to talk with him. Perhaps you can find out."

Some of the people of Jerusalem had told lies about Paul. They had made so much fuss that the Roman soldiers put Paul in prison. Paul had said that Jesus was alive, even though He had been put to death. But his enemies said Jesus was dead. They even wanted to kill Paul to keep him quiet.

Governor Felix had talked with Paul. But he couldn't find anything wrong with him.

Then Festus became governor. He talked with Paul, too. But he couldn't find anything wrong with him.

"I will talk with Paul tomorrow," said King Agrippa.

The next day King Agrippa marched into a big room with his friends. The Roman soldiers marched in, too. Trumpets blew. Flags waved. The king did everything he could to let the people know that he was the king.

"Bring in the prisoner!" the king ordered.

Everyone became quiet as Paul walked into the room. There was not a sound except the clanking of the chains on Paul's arms.

Paul walked bravely before the king. He stood tall and straight.

Then Governor Festus spoke. "This is the man I have told you about," he said. "Some people want to kill him. But I haven't found a thing wrong with him. Now he wants to be judged by the Emperor Caesar instead of his own people in Jerusalem. But what shall I tell Caesar when I send him there?"

The king looked at Paul. "Tell us about this," he said. "What is the problem?"

"Listen carefully to me," said Paul. "I will tell you why these people want to kill me."

Then Paul told how Jesus had talked with him from heaven. "He said that I should tell others that He is alive!" said Paul.

"You're crazy!" said Governor Festus.

"No, this is true," Paul answered. "King Agrippa knows about Jesus. He knows it's true."

King Agrippa moved nervously in his throne. He didn't want his friends to think that he believed in Jesus.

"You don't think I'm going to become a Christian because of what you're saying, do you?" the king asked.

"I wish you would," Paul answered bravely.

Everyone was amazed that Paul was speaking this way to the king. It took a lot of courage to tell the king that he should become a Christian. But he did.

"I wish all of you would become Christians," said Paul.

At last the meeting was over. King Agrippa walked out of the room with the governor.

"That man hasn't done anything wrong," said the king. "He shouldn't die because he believes in Jesus. If he hadn't asked to see Caesar, we could let him go out of prison."

"But he has asked," said Festus. "So we must send him."

King Agrippa and Governor Festus didn't want to send Paul to see Caesar in Rome. They knew that it was wrong. They felt sad that they must do it.

But Paul wasn't sad. Perhaps he could tell the Emperor Caesar himself about Jesus. Yes, he would stand there bravely and tell the Emperor that he, too, should become a Christian.

Paul was never ashamed to tell people that he believed in Jesus. He was never ashamed to tell them that they should become Christians, too.

WHAT DO YOU THINK?

1. How do you think Paul felt when he was brought before a king in chains? Did he beg for the king to set him free? What did he tell the king?
2. Was Paul ashamed to be a Christian? Why do you think that he wasn't? How did he show that he wasn't?
3. If you had been King Agrippa, what would you have thought of Paul's courage? Would you have wanted to free him? Why?

Mayor McBroom

"Mommi! Poppi! I won! I won!"

Maxi ran into the house so fast that he almost forgot to open the door. "I won the writing contest," he almost shouted to Mommi and Poppi.

"That's wonderful," said Poppi. "But you won that a month ago."

"No. No. No. That was our school contest. My teacher sent my essay to the city contest," said Maxi. "I won the contest for the whole city!"

Poppi and Mommi were excited now. It isn't every day that someone in the family wins a writing contest for the whole city.

"And guess what?" said Maxi. "Mayor McBroom has invited my family and teacher to be with me when he gives the award."

For the next two days the Muffin Family talked much about Maxi's meeting with the mayor. Maxi thought it was fun when someone called from the newspaper and asked him some questions.

"And they even said that a photographer would be there," Maxi told Mommi and Poppi. "They're going to put my picture in the paper."

Maxi was even more excited when the big day came for his meeting with Mayor McBroom. When he went with Mommi and Poppi and Mini into the mayor's office, there was his teacher. And there was the photographer and reporter from the newspaper. But most of all, there was Mayor McBroom himself.

"Well, well, well, Maxi," the mayor boomed. "Congratulations!" The mayor talked about the essay and how well Maxi had written about being friends with others.

"Maxi," said Mayor McBroom. "Tell me something about your very best friend. What kind of a person is he—or, heh, heh, heh—she?"

"My *very* best friend?" Maxi asked. Maxi thought for a moment. He knew what he wanted to say. But he looked around the room. There was the mayor and the reporter, and the photographer and his teacher. Maxi gulped. He WOULD say it.

"My *very* best friend is Jesus," said Maxi.

Maxi felt that everyone was staring at him. Should he have said that to the mayor? Would they print that in the newspaper? What would the mayor think of him now?

Then Mayor McBroom shook Maxi's hand. "Maxi, that was a very brave thing for you to say," the mayor told him. "I don't think anyone has ever said that to me before. But do you really mean it?"

"Of course," said Maxi. "Would you like to come with me to our church Sunday morning? Perhaps Jesus can become your best friend, too."

The mayor thought for a moment. Everyone was quiet, waiting to hear what the mayor would say.

"Maxi," the mayor said at last. "I haven't been to church for many years. But if Jesus means that much to you, I think I should go and find out why. It's a deal!"

As the mayor reached out to shake Maxi's hand again, the photographer took the picture. "We'll put that on page one," said the reporter. "Great story— contest winner invites mayor to church."

But Maxi was more excited that his new friend the mayor might meet his Best Friend, Jesus.

LET'S TALK ABOUT THIS
1. Why was it such a brave thing for Maxi to tell Mayor McBroom about Jesus before the others? Would you have done that?
2. How was Maxi like Paul before King Agrippa?
3. Are you ever afraid to tell others that Jesus is your best friend? What should you do when you are afraid?

Shipwreck!

ACTS 27

Paul was in trouble. He was on a ship, going to Rome. There he would be judged by the emperor or his officers. They could set him free. Or they could have him killed.

But Paul didn't worry about such things. He was too busy telling people about Jesus.

That was why Paul was a prisoner on a ship. His enemies didn't want him to tell others about Jesus. They told lies about him and had Roman soldiers arrest him. Now he had to go all the way to Rome to be judged.

But no matter what happened, Paul kept on saying what he thought God wanted him to say. Nobody could keep him from doing that.

"You must not sail this ship farther until next spring," Paul warned the ship's officers one day. Paul knew about the bad storms that came in the winter months in that part of the world.

The ship's officers knew about the bad storms, too. But they thought they knew more about sailing than Paul. They did not know that God was with Paul, helping him to say what he did.

"Don't tell us how to sail our ship!" they told Paul. Then they went on toward the next port.

But the winds began to blow when they were out on the sea. They blew faster and faster. Soon the waves rose up and beat against their ship. The sailors were afraid. The ship's officers were afraid, too.

"You should have listened to me!" Paul said bravely. He did not talk like a prisoner. He talked more like a commander. But that was because he knew that God was with him, even though he was in trouble.

Before long the ship was caught in a big storm. It blew the ship across the sea. The sailors could not stop it. They were so afraid. Perhaps they should have listened to Paul! Perhaps God was speaking to him!

"Listen to me!" Paul said one day. "An angel talked to me last night. He said that God promises none of you will die. But we will be shipwrecked on an island."

The sailors did listen to Paul now. They knew that God was with him. No man in trouble could talk that bravely unless God was with him.

For fourteen days the storm raged, beating against the ship. Then one night the sailors found that they were near land. Quickly they put out some anchors to keep the ship from blowing against the shore. Then they prayed that it would stay there until morning came and they could see what they were doing.

The next morning the sailors saw that they were near an island. The island had a bay in it.

"Let's try to get the ship in there," the sailors said.

But the ship ran into a sandbar and couldn't move, so it began to break into pieces. The sailors and the Roman soldiers became frightened.

"Kill the prisoners so they won't escape!" some Roman soldiers shouted.

"No!" said the commander of the soldiers. He did not want to kill Paul. He was afraid to kill a brave man who spoke for God.

Then the commander of the soldiers told everyone to jump into the water. He told them to swim on some boards to the island.

As the men swam toward the island, they must have thought of Paul. If only they were as brave as he was. Even though he was a prisoner, he spoke bravely for God. No matter what happened, Paul said what God wanted him to say.

Not one soldier or sailor was sure that he would have done the same. No, Paul had some special kind of courage that they didn't have. Perhaps they would find out more about it when they reached shore.

WHAT DO YOU THINK?

1. What do you think the soldiers and sailors thought of Paul? Why do you think they admired him?
2. How did Paul show that he was brave? Why do you think he spoke so bravely, even though he was in trouble?
3. What would the soldiers and sailors have thought of Paul if he had been afraid to say what God wanted? How would things have changed if he had blamed God for his trouble?

Play Ball!

Maxi had never played ball with BoBo before. He knew that BoBo was bigger and he was smaller, but he wasn't sure how BoBo played. Of course, BoBo didn't know much about Maxi's ball game either.

"Sorry, kid," BoBo said to Maxi. "Not on my team. I'm going for the big guys."

But Pookie knew better. He had played with Maxi before. "Come on our team, Maxi," said Pookie. "BoBo will be sorry when we get through with his team."

BoBo laughed when he heard that. "We'll see," he said. "We'll see."

"You pitch, Maxi," said Pookie. "Show BoBo how to play ball."

Maxi smiled and stepped up to the pitcher's mound. BoBo picked up a bat and stepped up to the plate.

"You'd better duck, Maxi," BoBo shouted. "I'm going to send it right through 'ya."

Maxi didn't answer. Instead he wrapped his fingers around the ball and let it fly. BoBo swung wildly at the ball as it sailed by.

"STEEERIKE ONE!" shouted the umpire.

"Must be a hole in my bat," BoBo growled. "This time I'll knock it over the fence."

"STEEERIKE TWO!" shouted the umpire.

"Dumb ball," BoBo growled. "Must be my bad day."

Maxi would up and threw again. BoBo wasn't even close to this one.

"STEEERIKE THREE!" shouted the umpire. "YOU'RE OUT!"

The next batter got two strikes, then lobbed a ball to Maxi, who threw it to first for the out. Another batter hit a fly ball to second base for the third out.

By this time BoBo had quieted down. But things kept on going that way. Late in the game BoBo made one run, which made him feel better. But it was too late. Maxi's team had won with six runs.

When the game was over, BoBo ran over to see Maxi. "Hey, Maxi, where did you learn to play ball like THAT?" he asked.

"Oh, it's just something I picked up in our church Peanut League," Maxi said calmly.

"Could I get in it?" BoBo asked.

"Sure, but the best part is not learning to play ball," Maxi told him.

BoBo looked puzzled. "It isn't?" he asked. "What else is there?"

"The most important thing is what we learn about Jesus," said Maxi. "So be there in Sunday school Sunday morning and we'll talk with the coach. OK?"

BoBo gulped. "Sure, Maxi, whatever you say," he said. "I'll be there."

1. How did Maxi use his talents to tell a friend about Jesus? How can you do that, too?
2. Was Maxi afraid to tell a bigger friend about Jesus? Should you ever be afraid to tell others, even "bigger" people about Jesus? Why not?

109

The Man
Who Was Not Afraid

ACTS 28

It really wasn't a very good time to be happy. Paul and some other men had been on a ship, going to Rome. But a great storm had come and driven their ship across the seas. Now the ship was wrecked and the men had paddled to the island on boards.

The men were cold and wet. Even the sky was cold and wet, for it was gloomy and raining.

"Let's find some dry wood and make a fire!" Paul suggested. A fire would help to warm them, so the men began to carry wood.

But as Paul threw some sticks into the fire, a poisonous snake sank its fangs into his hand. The men all stared at Paul.

"Snake!" some said.

"He will die!" said others.

But Paul wasn't afraid of the snake. He shook it into the fire and went on carrying sticks. The men kept watching him, certain that he would die soon.

"The snake bit him!" they said. "But he isn't dying! He isn't even afraid of it!"

Now the men knew that there was something special about Paul. They knew that God was with him.

When the governor of the island found that these men had been shipwrecked, he invited them all to his house for breakfast. Then he asked them to stay with him to eat lunch and dinner, too.

But Paul wanted to do something for God while he was there. When he heard that the governor's father was sick, he went to see him.

"I will pray for your father," Paul told the governor. When he did, God made the governor's father well again.

Before long, others on the island heard what had happened. They came to see Paul, too, for many of them were sick and wanted to be well. Paul was never too busy to see them. No matter how many came to see him, Paul took time to pray for them and God made them well.

But one day it was time to say good-bye. The soldiers had found another ship. It was time to take Paul to Rome. It was time for him to be judged.

Paul was not afraid to go. He knew that God would be with him in Rome as He had been with him during the shipwreck.

The people of the island were so happy that Paul had helped them. They brought many good gifts for Paul and the others. But they were sorry that their friend had to be judged in Rome. They were sure that such a brave, kind man had not done anything wrong.

So the brave man who had helped others sailed away from the island. Nobody knew what would happen to him in Rome. Of course, Paul did not know what would happen there, either. But he was sure that God would be with him. So why should he be afraid?

WHAT DO YOU THINK?

1. Why do you think Paul was not afraid of trouble? Why didn't he get angry at God when so many things went wrong?

2. Why did the people of the island come to Paul for help? Who gave Paul the power to help them?

3. Did Paul have reason to be afraid as he sailed away from the island? Why wasn't he?

Barking Dogs and Banana Peelings

"Do you really have to do it?" Maria asked.

"Yes," said Mini. "I promised my Sunday school teacher I would. Anyway, if I give fifty of these invitations to fifty families, several of them may come to our special program."

"But think of the fun we could have playing this afternoon," Maria complained.

"Sorry, Maria, a promise is a promise," said Mini. "You don't have to go with me if you want to play."

Maria mumbled some more and went down the street behind Mini as Mini rang the first doorbell. "Here is a special invitation to our Family Day at Sunday school," Mini said sweetly. "This paper will tell you about it."

"Thank you," the lady answered. "We will certainly look it over."

"That was fun," Mini said as they went down the walk. "Now we'll go to another house."

But Mini was only halfway up the walk to the next house when a big hairy dog came bounding toward her. "AROOF. AROOF. AROOF-AROOF-AROOF," went the dog.

"Run for your life!" shouted Maria.

"Not me," said Mini. "Nice doggie. Why don't you go find a bone somewhere?"

The dog stopped barking and began to wag its tail. Then he slurped Mini's hand with his long, wet tongue.

Mini gave the lady at the door an invitation and then headed for the next house. "Mini!" said Maria. "I'm scared. Let's go home."

"Not me," said Mini. "You may go if you wish. But I want to finish these—YIIIIK."

Mini's feet went flying into the air and she landed in a heap on the grass beside the walk. The forty-eight invitations were scattered around her.

"A banana peeling!" Maria said with disgust. "Who would ever leave a banana peeling on their front walk? Let's not give them an invitation."

"Sorry, Maria," said Mini. "They need it too." So Mini picked up the forty-eight invitations and headed for the door.

Later that afternoon, Maria and Mini were passing Pop's Sweet Shop. Who should be coming down the street but Mini's Sunday school teacher.

"Mini!" said the teacher. "How glad I am to see you. I was just going to buy an ice cream sundae. Will you and your friend join me?"

"Thank you," said Mini. "That sounds good right now. We're tired."

The teacher smiled as they sat down to eat the sundaes. "I see you're giving out our invitations," she said. "How are you doing?"

"Let's see," said Mini. "I've given out thirty-three invitations so far."

"And we've had six barking dogs, one banana peeling, one roller skate, and two sprinklers," Maria complained. "And I'm scared."

"Then why do you go with Mini?" asked the teacher.

Maria thought for a moment. "I guess if Mini can do it, I can. Anyway, she's my best friend."

"Aren't you afraid, too, Mini?" the teacher asked.

Mini took a big lick of ice cream and thought for a moment. "A little," she said. "But Jesus' friends shouldn't quit because of some old barking dogs and banana peelings, should they?"

LET'S TALK ABOUT THIS
1. When we're doing something for Jesus, why should we keep on working, even when we want to quit?
2. Why do you think Mini kept doing the work she had promised? Why didn't she quit? How was Mini like Paul?

WITH HARP AND SLING

The Shepherd Boy Who Became a King

1 SAMUEL 16:1-13

"That's enough!" the Lord told Samuel. "Stop feeling sorry for King Saul!"

Samuel had helped Saul become king. He had anointed him by pouring olive oil on his head. This showed people that God had chosen Saul to be king. Then he told the people of Israel to obey their king.

But Saul did not obey God. He tried to do things his own way. So God told Samuel that He would not let Saul be king much longer. Of course, this made Samuel feel very sad. He was sorry that their king did not please God.

"Take some olive oil to Bethlehem," God told Samuel. "You will anoint one of Jesse's sons to be Israel's new king some day."

"But Saul will kill me if he hears that I am going to do this," said Samuel.

"He must not find out what you are going to do," the Lord answered. "Take a young cow with you to Bethlehem and tell the people that you have come to make an offering to the Lord. Invite Jesse to be with you for this offering and I will show you which of his sons will be the next king."

Samuel did what the Lord told him. He always obeyed God.

When Samuel came to Bethlehem, some of the
leaders of the city came running to meet him. "Why is
the great Samuel coming to see us?" they wondered.
"What have we done wrong?"

"You haven't done anything wrong," Samuel told
them. "I have brought this young cow here to make a
sacrifice to the Lord. Get ready and come with me to
make this offering."

Jesse and his seven sons came with the leaders, too.
Eliab was a tall, handsome young man, the oldest of
the brothers. When Samuel saw him, he was sure that
God would choose him to be the next king.

"I don't choose kings because they are tall or handsome," God told Samuel. "That's the way you people
choose your leaders, but I don't. I look inside, to find
what a man thinks about Me. Eliab is not the one I
want."

Next, Jesse's son Abinadab came to Samuel. But
God did not choose him to be king either.

Jesse called Shammah and told him to go to
Samuel. But the Lord did not want Shammah to be
king.

Jesse sent each of his seven sons before Samuel. But
God did not want any of them to be king.

"The Lord did not choose any of your seven sons," Samuel told Jesse. "Is there another?"

"Yes, but he is only a lad," said Jesse. "He's out in the fields, taking care of my sheep."

"Bring him here!" Samuel ordered. "We will not eat until he comes."

While everyone waited, a servant ran to the fields to find the young shepherd lad. Before long, the boy came before Samuel.

"This is the one!" God told Samuel. "He will become the next king of Israel."

"Tell me your name," said Samuel.

"David," the lad answered.

"You will be Israel's next king, David," Samuel told him. "God has chosen you for this special work. He knows that you will obey Him."

When Samuel said this, he poured olive oil from an animal horn onto David's head. This was called anointing. It showed that God had chosen the young man for a special work.

The Spirit of God came upon young David at that very moment. From then on, young David had special power from God. God was with him, for He knew that David would obey Him and do the things that pleased Him.

WHAT DO YOU THINK?

1. Why did God say that Saul could not be king very long? What had he done?

2. Why do you think God chose David to be the next king instead of King Saul? Why did He choose David instead of his older brothers?

3. What happened to David when he was anointed? Why would this make him a better king?

A Special Person's Special Work

"Poppi."

"Yes, Mini?"

"Why is Mommi such a good cook?"

"Because she has special people to cook for, like you and Maxi."

"And you, Poppi?"

"Uh huh."

"But Mommi sews so well, too. How can she do that, too?"

"Because she has special people to sew for, I suppose."

"Like Maxi and me? And you, too?"

"Uh huh."

"Poppi."

"Uh huh."

"Mommi works hard to keep the house clean and wash the dishes and take us to music lessons and sit with us when we practice and things, doesn't she?"

"Uh huh."

"But why does she do all this for us? Why doesn't she make us do it?"

"I guess because we're special people to her, Mini. We like to do things for special people, don't we? In fact, it's fun to do special things for special people, isn't it?"

"Poppi."

"Yes, Mini?"

"Is Mommi a special person, too?"

"Yes, Mini. Very special."

"Then it should be fun to do special things for her, too, shouldn't it?"

"Uh huh."

"Poppi."

"Yes, Mini?"

"Does it take a special person to be a mommi?"

"Yes, Mini. Being a mommi is a special kind of work. God made it that way. So He has special kinds of people do His mommi work."

"Is my mommi a special kind of person for her mommi work?"

"Yes, Mini. Very special."

"Then I should thank God for my special mommi, shouldn't I?"

"Yes, Mini. You should. Do you want to now?"

LET'S TALK ABOUT THIS

1. Why is being a mommi special work? Who made it that way?

2. How did people show a Bible-time king that God had chosen him for His special work? How was the king's work like a mommi's work? Were both special? Were both chosen by God to do their special work?

3. In what way is your work special? Do you want to make it more special? Then do your work for special people and for God.

A Harp for the King

1 SAMUEL 16:14-23

The Lord wanted to help Saul be a good king. But King Saul wanted to do things his own way. He would not listen to God. He would not obey God. At last God's Spirit left Saul and went away.

Then another spirit came to live with Saul. This was an evil spirit who made Saul feel sad. He made Saul do things he did not really want to do.

Before long Saul began to scream at his servants and say terrible things to his friends. The people in Saul's palace knew that they should talk with Saul about these things. But who could tell a king that he was behaving like a madman?

At last some of Saul's servants thought of a plan. "How would you like some music when the evil spirit bothers you?" they said timidly.

The servants were sure that King Saul would scream at them or throw something at them. But he didn't. He thought this was a good idea, for he knew that he needed it.

"We will find someone who plays the harp," the servants said. "When you hear the harp music, you will feel better."

"Good!" said the king.

The servants tried to think of the kind of harp player that their king should have. He must be brave and handsome and strong. And he must play the harp well. What more could they ask?

Then one of the servants remembered. "I know a young man who can play for the king," he said. "He is brave and handsome and strong. And he plays the harp well."

"Good!" said the other servants. "He has everything!"

"He has even more," said the first servant. "Best of all, the Lord is with him."

"Who is he?" the others asked.

"David, Jesse's son!" said the servant. "He lives in Bethlehem."

Before long, messengers were on their way to Jesse's home in Bethlehem. They must find young David and ask him to play for his king.

"Your son will live in the palace with the king," the messengers told Jesse. "He will calm the king when the evil spirit comes to visit him."

Jesse was pleased that his young son could help the king. That was an honor.

David was pleased, too. He was happy that he could play his harp to calm the king.

David had never played his harp for a king before. He had always played his sweet music for his father's sheep while he watched them on the hillsides. David made many songs and played them for his sheep. But would this music be good enough for the king? David didn't know, but he would do his best.

"Wait!" Jesse said to the king's messengers. "I must send a gift to my king. You will take it back with you." Jesse wanted to do his best for his king, too.

Jesse began shouting orders to his servants.

"Bring a donkey!"

"Fill a skin with our best wine!"

"Get some loaves of bread for the king!"

Before long, Jesse had a fine gift for the king. He would send a donkey loaded with food and wine and a young goat. The messengers left for Saul's palace with all the good gifts. Young David went, too, carrying his harp that he would play for the king.

How happy the king was to hear David's beautiful music! The sweet notes and words of David's psalms soothed his troubled spirit. So Saul honored David by making him his own armor bearer.

"Let David stay with me," Saul begged Jesse. "Let him live here in the palace and help me."

For a long time, David stayed in the palace with the king, playing and singing for him. Many of these songs were probably the same psalms that you read in your Bible.

As time passed, the Philistines began to fight Saul and his people. They brought great armies and chariots. So Saul had to leave his palace and take his armies to fight the Philistines, the enemies of his people. He did not have time to listen to harp music now.

So David went home to Bethlehem to care for his father's sheep again and protect them from the wild animals. Once more he sat with them on the hillsides, playing his harp and singing sweet songs that he once sang to the king. As he did, David often remembered how he had done his best to help his king.

WHAT DO YOU THINK?

1. Why did the king need someone to play a harp for him? Would he have needed this music if the Lord had been with him?

2. Why did the king's servants choose David to play for the king? Why do you think King Saul liked David's music so well?

3. Why do you think David wanted to do his best for King Saul? What happened when David did his best for his king? How might the story change if David had not tried to do his best?

Sweet Music

"Maxi!"

"What?"

"Have you practiced your music today?"

"No, Mommi."

"When do you plan to do it?"

"Later."

That's the way it had been for several days. Maxi liked to play his guitar. But he didn't like to practice. But Maxi is like many girls and boys, isn't he?

Maxi was still thinking about "later" when Poppi came home. "Did you hear who's going to be on TV tonight?" Poppi asked Maxi.

"Yeah, Gordon Hotfoot!" said Maxi. "He's fantastic!"

"Are you going to watch him?" asked Poppi.

"Of course," said Maxi. "Some day I'm going to be a great guitar player like him."

"Perhaps," said Poppi. "He's supposed to tell a little about himself tonight. He may tell you how to do it."

Maxi could hardly wait until the Gordon Hotfoot program was on. He was the first one before the TV.

"Listen to him play," said Maxi. "I'm going to be like him some day."

At last Gordon Hotfoot stopped playing. He ran his fingers softly over the strings. "Some of you out there are just learning to play," he said. "I want to tell you two secrets."

"Here it is!" said Maxi. "That's for me."

"First, be sure to practice every day," said Gordon. "Do it again and again until you do it just right."

Maxi gulped when he heard that. He tried not to look at Mommi, but he noticed that she was smiling.

"Second," said Gordon. "When you get ready to play, think of the most important person you know. Play for that person."

After the program Maxi ran to get his guitar. "I'm going to practice at least a half hour every day," said Maxi. "And I'm going to play for the most important person I know."

"Who is that?" asked Mini Muffin.

"Jesus," said Maxi. "If I can play for Him, I will always do my very, very best."

LET'S TALK ABOUT THIS
1. What two things did Maxi learn about some ways to do his best in music?
2. Do you think these two things helped David play sweet music for King Saul? Why is it important to play or sing or use other talents for Jesus? How can He help us use them?

The Little Stone
That Won a Battle

1 SAMUEL 17:1-53

"Take this bread and grain to your brothers," said David's father. "And here is some cheese for their captain."

David wished that he could be in the army of Israel with his brothers. He would rather fight the Philistines than take care of his father's sheep. But everyone said that he was too young.

"I'm not too young to kill lions and bears when they try to catch our sheep!" David thought. But he knew that someone had to care for the sheep. Since he was the youngest of Jesse's boys, then he must do it.

"Be sure to bring us some word from your brothers," said Jesse. "We want to know how things are going."

Early the next morning David left for the Valley of Elah where the army of Israel was camped. He arrived just as the soldiers were leaving for the battlefield.

"This food is for my brothers and their captain," David told the man who took care of those things.

David left the food with the man and ran off to find his brothers. He had just started to talk with them when a shout came from the other side of the little stream.

"Send a man to fight me!" a voice cried out to the men of Israel.

"Who is that man?" David whispered to his brothers.

"Goliath of Gath!" they answered.

Goliath was the biggest man David had ever seen. He was over nine feet tall, wore a great suit of armor, and carried a spear that weighed over twenty-five pounds.

When Goliath shouted, the soldiers of Israel began to tremble. This made David angry.

"He can't talk to God's people like that!" said David. "What is he trying to do?"

Then Goliath shouted again. "If I kill your man, you will be our slaves," he said. "But if your man kills me, then we will be your slaves."

"He's too big for us to fight!" said a soldier. "He has been saying this for forty days, but no one will go over there to fight him."

"I'll fight him!" said David.

When David's older brother Eliab heard that, he was angry. "Go back home and take care of the sheep!" he grumbled. "You're just a little kid who wants to see us get into a fight."

But some of the soldiers had heard what David said. They took him to see King Saul.

"I'll fight that Philistine giant!" David told the king.

"But you're too young," Saul answered. "You could never fight him and win."

"I have fought lions and bears with only a club and my slingshot," said David. "The Lord saved me from them and He will save me from that giant."

Saul thought about that. No one else in his army would fight Goliath. Perhaps this young fellow could win.

"You may do it," said the king. "May the Lord help you."

Then King Saul gave David his armor to wear. "This will protect you from the giant," he said. But when David put on the king's armor, he could not walk or run.

"God will protect me from the giant," he said. "I do not need this armor. He will help me use my club and slingshot."

David picked up five smooth stones from the little stream that ran between the two armies. Then he walked toward Goliath with only his club and slingshot.

"What do you think I am, a dog?" Goliath roared when he saw David. "You came here to fight the great Goliath with a club? I'll feed you to the birds and wild animals."

"I come in the name of the Lord, our God," David shouted back. "You have only your sword and spear to help you, but I have the Lord to help me. When I feed you and your friends to the birds and animals, our soldiers will learn that the Lord doesn't need swords and spears to fight His battles."

When David said that, he reached into the little bag he carried and took out one of the stones. Then he put it into his slingshot. Around and around he whirled the slingshot, and sent the stone flying toward Goliath.

With a cry, Goliath sank to the ground. When the Philistines saw that, they were afraid and began to run away. Then the army of Israel went after them and chased them all the way home.

The battle was won with a little stone. But most of all, it was won with the Lord's help.

WHAT DO YOU THINK?

1. Why did a young lad try to fight a giant with only a slingshot and a club? What did he have that was better than the giant's sword and spear?
2. Why did David have more courage than all the soldiers of Israel? Where did he get such courage?
3. How do you think the army of Israel felt after the battle? How might the Philistines have felt then about God?

Big Bill Bluffalo

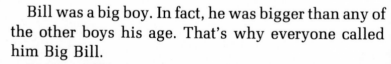

Bill was a big boy. In fact, he was bigger than any of the other boys his age. That's why everyone called him Big Bill.

But Big Bill was a tease. He liked to tease the girls and pretend to be tough with the boys. Most of the boys and girls let Big Bill get by with this, even though they knew that he was bluffing.

"Big Bill is a bluff," some of the boys and girls would say.

"Big Bill is like a big buffalo," said others.

So the boys and girls began calling him Big Bill Bluffalo.

One day Maxi and Mini were walking toward home when Big Bill stepped in front of them. "Sorry, twerps," he said. "This street is closed. You'll have to detour."

"But our house is down there," said Mini. "We want to go home."

"The street is closed!" Bill growled.

"Hey, you can't do that!" Maxi argued. "This is our street, too. We aren't going to walk four blocks to get home."

"Yes! Today you are," said Big Bill. "So get going!"

"Let's go, Maxi," Mini whispered. "Let's ask God to help us with old Bluffalo."

Big Bill must have wondered why Mini and Maxi stopped for several minutes to close their eyes and whisper. He must have wondered even more when they ran down the street laughing.

"Dumb kids," Big Bill growled. "Why are they so happy about all this? I don't like it."

Big Bill didn't like it later when he saw Maxi and Mini come back. And he certainly didn't like what he saw with them.

"Buster, come down here and meet Big Bill Bluffalo!" said Maxi. "Big Bill says we're not going home. We say we are! What do you say?"

Buster poked his big cold nose into Big Bill's face. "RRRROWWR," he said.

"Wh—what did he say?" asked Big Bill, not looking very big now.

"He says he thinks it's time for you to go home," said Maxi. "Right now!"

"I—I was just going," said Big Bill, looking more nervous all the time. "See you later everybody! Bye."

"Time for us to go home, too," said Maxi. "You first, Buster."

"RRRROWWR," said Buster.

"What did he say?" asked Mini.

"He says Big Bill isn't so big after all," said Maxi. "Right, Buster?"

"RRRROWWR!"

LET'S TALK ABOUT THIS

1. What kind of help did Maxi and Mini need when they met Big Bill?

2. What two kinds of help did they get? How do you think God helped them? How did Buster help them?

3. In the Bible story, how did God help David? How did David's sling help him?

4. In what way would you like for God to help you today? Will you ask Him?

Good Friends

1 SAMUEL 17:55—18:4

Young David had just saved the army of Israel. With the Lord's help and his slingshot, he had killed the Philistine giant Goliath and frightened the army of the Philistines away.

"What do you know about that young man's family?" King Saul asked General Abner.

"Nothing," said the general.

"Then find out all you can!" the king ordered.

Saul had promised that the man who killed Goliath would marry his daughter. Now that David had killed the giant, the king wanted to know all he could about his new son-in-law and his family.

Abner hurried out to find David. He brought the young man to see the king.

"Tell me about your family," said the king.

"My father is Jesse," David answered. "Our home is at Bethlehem."

David was from a poor family. His father Jesse was only a shepherd. A shepherd boy did not usually marry a princess.

"Not one of my soldiers is as brave as you," said the king. "You were the only one brave enough to fight Goliath."

While King Saul talked with David, Prince Jonathan sat nearby, listening. Jonathan was a brave young man. Once he had attacked the whole Philistine army by himself, with only his armor-bearer with him. He saw what a brave young man David was, too. How good it would be to have such a brave friend! He was glad that David would be living with him at the palace.

At last the king stopped talking with David. When David left Saul, Jonathan went with him.

"I want to be your best friend," Jonathan told David. "I want to be like a brother. I promise that I will be your friend as long as I live."

Jonathan gave David his beautiful cloak. A prince did not usually give his cloak to people. What a great honor it was when he did!

"Here is my sword, my armor, my bow, and my belt," Jonathan said. "These gifts will show my friendship to you."

"I have no good gifts such as these to give," said David. "But I give you my word that I will always be your friend."

So David and Jonathan agreed that they would never hurt each other. As long as they lived, they would always be good friends and help each other.

And that's what good friends should do, shouldn't they?

WHAT DO YOU THINK?

1. How did Jonathan show David that he wanted to be a good friend? How did David show Jonathan that he wanted to be his good friend?
2. How long did Jonathan and David plan to be friends? What did this mean that they would do for one another?

The Friend I Never Saw

"Mommi, do you have any friends you've never seen?"

"I suppose, Mini. Like who?"

"Oh, like someone far away. Perhaps across the ocean."

"Hmmmm. Let me think, Mini. I really don't believe I do have a friend like that."

"Mommi, may I have a friend across the ocean?"

"I suppose, Mini. Who are you thinking of?"

"The girl in this picture. My Sunday school teacher says she doesn't have enough food to eat or clothes to wear."

"Hmmm. She really does need some friends, then, doesn't she, Mini?"

"Yes, Mommi. And our Sunday school class is going to help her. Some of us are giving half of our allowance all summer for her."

"Are you, Mini?"

"If it's OK with you, Mommi."

"I think that would be wonderful, Mini. But are you sure you want to do it?"

"Yes, Mommi. I don't want to give up my money, but I want to help my new friend."

"Will you write to her?"

"Oh, yes, Mommi. I want to tell her about my friend."

"Your friend? Which one, Mini?"

"You know. My friend Jesus. Perhaps she will ask Him to become her friend, too."

"Then she would have *two* new friends, Mini. That is even better than one friend."

"That's what I thought, too, Mommi. Oh thank you, Mommi."

"For what, Mini?"

"For being my mommi and knowing how I feel."

LET'S TALK ABOUT THIS

1. What should someone do when a friend needs help? What does Jesus do when we need help and we ask Him?

2. What kinds of help did the girl across the ocean need? What kind of help did Mini want to give? What kind of help could Jesus give?

3. Does someone need you for a friend? How can you help that person? Why would it help most by telling about your friend Jesus?

Mini's Word List

Twelve words that all Minis and Maxis want to know.

ANOINT — An important person, such as a king, was anointed to show that God had chosen him for a special work. A man of God, such as a priest or prophet, poured olive oil on the person's head. This was called anointing.

ARMOR-BEARER — An armor-bearer carried the armor, such as a shield and helmet, for a king or great warrior. Goliath had an armor-bearer. At one time, David was King Saul's armor-bearer.

CAESAR — Caesar is the title for the man who ruled the Roman Empire. During the time of Christ, Israel was part of the Roman Empire.

DISCIPLE — Someone who follows another person and lives by his teachings is a disciple. Jesus had many disciples, but He chose twelve of them to do His special work.

HARP — A wooden musical instrument with strings, shaped something like a U is called a harp. David played this kind of harp for King Saul.

HEAVEN — Heaven is the place where Jesus lives with God. Those who love Jesus and accept Him as Saviour will live there with Him forever.

JEW — A Jew is a descendant of Abraham, Isaac, and Jacob. God had spoken to these three men, promising to be with them and their people.

OFFERING — An offering was a gift for God. Sometimes the gift was meat, burned on an altar.

PHILISTINES — The Philistines were enemies of Israel who lived in the flat country near the sea. They often fought Israel during the time of David and Saul.

SHEPHERD — A shepherd took care of sheep. Jesus called Himself a shepherd and His people sheep because He takes care of them with the love and protection that a shepherd gives to his sheep.

SLING — A sling was a piece of leather with a string tied to each end. To use it, one would put a stone in the leather, hold the ends of the string, and whirl it around and around. Then he would let one string go, sending the stone flying.

TEMPT — When something or someone tries to get us to do bad things, we are tempted. That means we may want to do it, even though we know it is wrong.